UNIQUELY INFUSED OLIVE OIL RECIPES

UNIQUELY INFUSED OLIVE OIL RECIPES

R&O RANCH
Ian Overton & Kesha Rogers

CONTENTS

CHAPTER 1

Welcome

Thank you for buying our recipe book! The R&O Ranch was founded as a husband and wife team in the spring of 2023, in Johnson City, Tennessee. We wrote this book because we believe that healthy food should taste amazing, and more people would eat well if they knew how to make their food taste better. There is a widespread desire among many people to return to methods popular before the rise of packaged microwave dinners and fast food drive thrus, in what might simply be termed a homesteading lifestyle: fresh, local, whole foods that are free of artificial ingredients and toxic pesticides, seasoned and preserved using time tested methods rather than modern chemicals.

This book was primarily written for four types of people:

1. **The Foodie:** You want food to taste amazing, and you want to improve your technique so you can impress your tastebuds, your friends, and your sweetie. If the food is healthy and nutritious that's a bonus, but if not that's not a deal breaker.

2. **The Health Nut:** You want to eat right, and enjoy a life free from the achy body and diseases that everyone else seems to be getting. Being called a health nut is a personal compliment, and you are unashamed in your pursuit of *pura vida*, yet you'd also like your food to taste great.

3. **The Busy Cook:** It's a weeknight, and you don't have time to spend 3 hours in the kitchen making a masterpiece. Simple ingredients should be easy to prepare, fuel the body and mind, and be on the table with enough time to relax for the meal together.

4. **The Gift Giver:** Maybe you aren't these people (yet) but you have that sister, uncle, spouse, or friend who is. You just know they would appreciate some good olive oil and ideas on how to use it.

Chances are, you may be all of these people. If that's true, do we have a treat in store for you!

52 Recipes Featuring Uniquely Infused Olive Oils

SAUCES AND SALSAS

VEGETABLE SIDE DISHES

SALADS

FISH, MEAT AND EGGS

SNACKS AND DESSERTS

CHAPTER 2

Uniquely Infused
Olive Oils

If you're a Busy Cook, feel free to skip ahead to the recipes. Foodies and Health Nuts keep reading...

Sometimes we have to state the obvious: to make quality food, you need to start with quality ingredients. So we start with the highest quality oil on the planet, which is Extra Virgin Olive Oil (EVOO). What is it? Virgin and Extra Virgin are designators for olive oils that are made by mechanically crushing and separating the oils from the olive fruit without heating the plant above 27C/80.6⁰ F, or treating it with other chemicals. Both Virgin and Extra Virgin olive oils are "cold pressed" in this way. An olive oil cannot be labeled as Virgin or Extra Virgin if it contains any oils extracted using heat or chemicals. Extra Virgin meets the highest standards for taste and quality, and is the highest grade of olive oil available. According to the American Olive Oil Producers Association, extra virgin olive oil is preferred over other oils because it has not been refined with heat or chemicals that introduce impurities or degrade its quality.

This being said, just like wine, there are many varieties of EVOO, due to the diversity of microclimate growing areas and different subspecies grown across the world. They have a wide range of flavor qualities, ranging from fruity, grassy, peppery, astringent and mild. They have a wide range of colors, from dark green to pale yellow. These factors also influence the polyphenol content of the oil. Typically, the higher the phenol count, the more astringent and peppery the taste. We will talk more about polyphenols and other chemistry later.

Generally speaking, olive oil should be consumed within 2 years of being harvested. It does degrade over time with exposure to high heat, sunlight, water and oxygen. This can happen faster with lower grades of oil.

INFUSING YOUR OWN OILS

So you want to make your own infused olive oils? Great! Before we talk about the right way (sous vide), let's explain why the other ways are wrong. Feel free to skip down to the Sous Vide Method section below if you're impatient.

The internet is replete with cooking blogs filled with Instagram-worthy-but-totally-unsafe stock images of oil stuffed with sprigs of fresh herbs. These articles generally describe how to make non-shelf stable, highly perishable infusions that must be kept in a refrigerator. What are the enemies of olive oil? High heat, sunlight, water and oxygen. Fresh herbs and spices introduce two risks: food borne pathogens like botulism or wild yeasts, and the introduction of water and oxygen.

Botulism is naturally present in the ground, meaning it is frequently present in raw garlic. It thrives in the anaerobic environment of the oil at room temperatures. Keeping food refrigerated prevents it from multiplying, and cooking food above 250^0 F kills the spores. Botulism is a potent poison. You don't want it. This is why many states prohibit the sale of oils infused with fresh garlic. Unfortunately, refrigerating your oil means it will solidify, so you have to leave it out on the counter in order to use it.

Many fresh herbs, especially those grown outside, will have wild yeasts or other microscopic spores on them. Introducing these to your food can impart unpleasant flavors, and increase spoilage rates. You can sterilize your fresh herbs by soaking them in a solution of 1 tablespoon of citric acid powder per every 3 cups of water for 24 hours. When you pour out the water, you'll see it tinted from the color of your herbs. This is you pouring some of their flavor down the drain. Your formerly "fresh" herbs are now also soaking wet, so you will need to dry them to avoid introducing water into your oil. What a hassle! Putting fresh herbs in afterward "for looks" defeats the entire purpose of sanitizing them, and such oil needs to be refrigerated (after posting your Instagram photo, of course).

Active water content (measured as A_W) is a scale between 0 and 1.0 that measures how wet a food is. Water has an A_W of 1.0, while fresh fruits, vegetables and meats have an A_W rating between 0.93 and 0.99, while raisins, honey, dried fruits, and meat jerky is typically in the range of 0.50 to 0.65. According to the University of Tennessee's Institute of Agriculture, for a food to be rated as not requiring temperature controls (such as refrigeration or heating) it needs to have an A_W rating below 0.88 or be acidified. The Food Untold places that limit at 0.60, as illustrated above in the graph adapted from their article "Water Activity (A_W) and Food Safety".

Dehydrated herbs and spices will have an Aw content in the range of 0.2, and that is why we recommend using them instead of fresh ingredients.

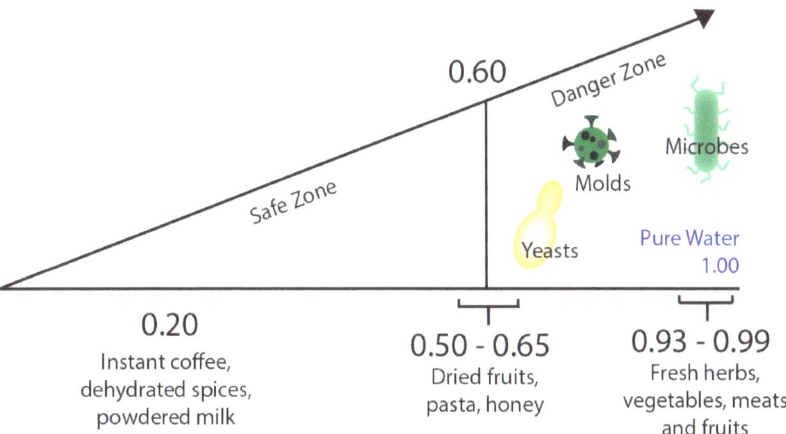

The popular methods described on the internet tell you to heat your oil to an imprecise temperature (before it starts to smoke around 350° F, when it's "shimmering", when it's "hot"), add your flavors, let them cook for 5 to 10 minutes, then turn off the heat and let it soak for several hours. This method isn't precise enough to be reliably repeatable, risks scorching your ingredients, and exposes your olive oil to unnecessary heat and oxygen. Another method on the internet advises using the coffee "cold brew" method. How flavors are supposed to infuse into congealed EVOO over a week is beyond my patience to try. Enough with the amateurs, let's do this the right way.

THE SOUS VIDE METHOD

The superior method of infusion, which is the one used by R&O Ranch, is the sous vide method. If you aren't familiar, sous vide (pronounced Sue Veed) is French for "under vacuum". Ingredients are vacuum sealed in a plastic bag or glass container and placed in a water bath. An immersion circulator is a tool placed in the water that heats and circulates it at a precise temperature, slowly and gently poaching the ingredients.

This is superior because it extracts the most flavor out of dried herbs and spices, eliminates the danger of scorching or oxidizing your ingredients, and is reliably repeatable. You will want to experiment with time, temperatures and spice quantities to find a flavor combination that tastes good to you, but generally expect 3-4 hours around 160° F. Err on the side of whole leaves and seeds because they are easier to filter out later, and avoid powdered spices. You will likely notice some sediment depending on how powdery your ingredients are.

Depending on your budget, there are two ways to prepare your oil. The cheaper way is to mix your oil and spices into a silicone mold, freeze it solid overnight, and vacuum seal it in a plastic bag like you would a steak. Souper Cubes sells food grade silicone trays with lids in larger sizes that will easily pop your frozen oil block out and into your bag. As of this writing, a no-frills immersion circulator, silicone trays, a roll of bags, and a simple vacuum sealer will run you about $160. If you have more money to spend on equipment, consider investing in a vacuum chamber sealer, which will allow you to skip the freezing step.

After you have steeped your oil, you need to strain the solids out. The cheap but messy way is to squeeze the oil through a nut milk bag or drain it through several layers of cheesecloth until it drips dry. It's worth the time and money to invest in a fruit press and let a metal plate do the squeezing for you.

Before you bottle your oil, you must sanitize and completely dry your bottles and pouring equipment. If your dishwasher can't dry the inside of your bottles, you can put them upside down in your oven at 250^0 F for 20 minutes to sterilize them.

Infused oil prepared this way will store in your pantry the same as oil you purchase at the supermarket. It does not need to be refrigerated. Like all olive oils, you should consume it within 2 years from the date it was pressed.

IMPORTANT NOTE: FINISHING OILS

For reasons that will be made clear in the next chapter, we highly recommend using infused oils as a finishing oil in your meals, rather than as a starting oil. Why would you spend all this time and money to make a delicious oil only to cover up the flavors by adding lots of ingredients on top of it? For this reason, the recipes in this book focus on foods that don't need to be cooked, are cooked in a way that highlights the flavors of the oil, or have the oil added near or at the end.

CHAPTER 3

Olive Oil for Healthy Living

You've probably heard that olive oil is really good for you. Or maybe you are interested in a healthy lifestyle, but like so many of us are somewhat overwhelmed by what seems like loads of contradictory information out there. In this chapter, we will summarize what we believe to be a basis for a healthy lifestyle, and the important role that infused olive oil plays in a healthy diet. Rather than "live to eat" or "eat to live" we should "live to love." In our view, a life well lived looks back one day to realize it enjoyed over 90 years defined by laughter, good health, meaning, and memories with loved ones. It wasn't held captive by over-scrutinizing every calorie, fearing impending losses, or feeling isolated. Such a life of abundance is possible.

It is our view that there are five dynamic factors that work together to produce a life of abundance. These five factors are:

1. **Spiritual Purpose.** Many people today feel separated from God because the world is so riddled with ugliness. It would be lost, but God so loves the world that he sent Jesus Christ to pay off those debts and be a living role model for us on how to rediscover our spiritual purpose for living. We hope you understand the truth in these words, but if you are still seeking an ultimate purpose in your life, we invite you to read the good news found in the Bible. Establishing a personal spiritual purpose in life transforms suffering into virtue, gives you reasons not to give up, and encourages you to become better. To lack such purpose is to experience a living hell, and we don't wish that on anyone. Living a meaningful life directed from the highest connection, that of our soul to the creator of the universe, is the bedrock of a life of abundance, no matter how hard it gets.

2. **Family.** Our family is our core support network we rely on throughout our lives. We believe that people should get married, have kids or adopt them, and live near their extended families. Families should have projects together, focused around common hobbies, a shared spiritual purpose, raising children, and passing along values over the generations. Some people decry the nuclear family and seek its dissolution; that is a tragic mistake. Our family keeps us going, cares for us in our times of need, and motivates us to success.

3. **Community.** Humans are social creatures, but social media is not a replacement for real friends. The best experiences aren't measured by how many "likes" the "perfect" photo got, but in the camaraderie and bonding that happens by going through experiences together. Our community is where we live out our spiritual purpose. Much of society today is so atomized that people feel lonely in groups, don't have time to get together,

and don't know how to even make friends. Church, sports, and hobbies are easy ways to engage with a community.

4. **Exercise, Rest, and Play.** The human body is built to move, yet the modern American lifestyle has become mostly sedentary. There is a huge volume of evidence showing that continual, low intensity exercise throughout the day, with adequate sleep, and dedicated time reserved for play and enjoyment, all help maintain a body that is resistant to chronic diseases, inflammation, and achiness. Recurring cardiovascular exercise, strength training, and stretching, especially outside, are essential to longevity and health. If you want to lose weight, especially dangerous visceral fat around your organs, you need to be active while maintaining a slight calorie deficit below your base metabolic rate.

5. **Nutrition.** There are a number of healthy dietary choices out there that you can tailor to your body's unique needs, but all of them have this in common: 1) eat fresh whole, natural foods, not highly processed convenience foods full of sugar, preservatives, and artificial ingredients; 2) stop eating once you are about 80% full; 3) drink enough water. From there, you can pick the meal plan that works best for you. We personally recommend a meal plan that generally follows the Mediterranean Diet, which prioritizes fresh vegetables, beans, nuts, fruit, whole grains, and olive oil, supplemented with eggs, fatty fish, and occasionally beef and chicken.

Since this *is* a recipe book, we will focus on point number 5: eating a mostly vegetarian diet. We aren't just talking about salads here; beans, tree fruits, nuts, root vegetables, leafy greens, berries, herbs, corn, breads, and cheeses all meet this standard. Meat contains all nine essential proteins, with greater bioavailability than what's available through eating plants alone, and shouldn't be left out of your meal planning. The Mediterranean diet includes fatty fish and eggs. However you structure your meal plan, the emphasis here is to focus on fresh, whole foods prepared by hand, rather than microwave processed foods stuffed full of laboratory made salts, fats, sugars, preservatives, antibiotics, colorings and pesticides. And avoid the drive thru fast food lifestyle like the poison it is.

MAKING FOOD TASTY AGAIN

There is a saying among cooks, "Fat is where the flavor is." And we also know that a pinch or two of salt helps make flavors pop out and be noticed. But let's be honest, while vegetables, whole grains, and fruits contain essential nutrients, they typically are *not* where the fat or salt are. Ask any six year old whether they are more excited to eat a salad or a fried chicken nugget if you don't believe me. So the question becomes, how do we make a mostly vegetarian diet actually taste good? The answer is infused olive oil, *of course!* (You are reading an olive oil recipe book after all.)

At its most basic, cooking is the technique by which we use chemistry to make food taste good, smell good, and safe to eat. There are five major food flavor categories: salty, sweet, sour, bitter, and savory (also called umami), with sub-flavors like fatty or spicy (like raw garlic or ginger, rather than hot peppers). Vegetables primarily taste savory, bitter, or sour. Cooked grains will be slightly sweet. Fruit generally tastes sweet or sour depending on its sugar and citric acid content. Meats, dairy and nuts primarily taste savory and fatty, with a hint of sweetness. We change the chemistry and texture of these ingredients by adding heat, acids, salts, water, air, or fats to break down tissues, convert carbohydrates into sugars, create structure, and release or convey flavor.

Salt and carbohydrates readily dissolve in water, while they do not dissolve in fats. This is due to their chemical structure, specifically the presence of oxygen molecules and the bivalent nature of water. A single water molecule has two positively charged hydrogen atoms and one negatively charged oxygen atom. This creates a weak electrical field, which salt and carbohydrates bind with. When salt dissolves in water (as in your saliva) it reduces the sensation of bitterness and conveys electricity, which stimulates your nervous system to respond to the presence of your food. This is why we use the phrase "salt to taste" in recipes; not to taste salty, but to taste the flavors of your dish. Fats generally lack, or have very few oxygen molecules, and are electrically neutral. Instead, oils dissolve into other oils, such as the oil essences naturally present in your ingredients.

PLANT ESSENTIAL OILS

Terpenes are a broad class of plant hydrocarbons (hydrogen-carbon chains) that perform a wide range of essential functions for plants, such as protecting them from infection, helping them reproduce, and smelling and tasting good. A subcategory of terpenes are called terpenoids, which are also hydrocarbons but have a small amount of oxygen molecules present. These plant oils are volatile, meaning they evaporate and disperse through the air at room temperature. When you walk through the forest on a sunny day and take that deep relaxing breath full of fresh tree smell, you're breathing in their essential oils. We call these oils "essential", because they often contain the essence of the flavor we identify as tasty or medicinally useful.

None of our direct or implied statements about the benefits of essential oils are to be construed as medical advice, and will never be evaluated by the Food and Drug Administration. We are business owners and cooks, not doctors. Despite a plethora of scientific studies published about the health and dietary benefits of the Mediterranean diet, terpenes, polyphenols, sunlight and outdoor exercise, the FDA cannot and will never make statements about naturally occurring substances because naturally occurring substances cannot be trademarked, patented, or copyrighted. Please do your own research, form your own conclusions, and seek medical advice from professionals when appropriate.

OXIDATIVE STRESS VS. ANTI-OXIDANTS

Oxidative stress is a term that refers to the harmful effect that reactive oxygen (or reactive nitrogen) ions have on your body's cells. When oxygen (or nitrogen) molecules become ionized, it means they have an odd number of electrons; this makes them electrically unstable. These molecules are known as free radicals. Their electrical instability causes the free radical to seek an electron from its environment, such as the cells in your body.

When a free radical steals an electron from your cell to stabilize itself, it causes your own cell to become electrically unstable, so it seeks an electron from another nearby cell in your body. This cycle perpetuates until disrupted, and is called oxidative stress. The long term effects of oxidative stress contribute to premature aging, persistent inflammation, and the emergence or worsening of deadly and chronic diseases such as cancer, diabetes, multiple sclerosis, hardening of the arteries, dementia, hypertension, heart disease, cardiovascular disease, DNA damage, arthritis, and stroke.

Your body naturally produces free radicals as part of your immune, exercise and stress responses. In low amounts, free radicals play an important role in bodily health. However, if a person has suffered a long time with persistent trauma from abusive social environments at home, the effect of being in a heightened state of alertness and stress increases the prevalence of free radicals (among many other chemicals) in their body. If a person's immune system is under constant stress, their body produces more free radicals. If a person's job requires them to work long hours in a high stress environment, possibly without adequate time to calm down and decompress, their body produces more free radicals. If a person engages in very high intensity exercise, their body produces more free radicals in the recovery process.

EYES
Cataracts, Macular Degeneration, Retinal Degeneration

LUNGS
Allergies, Asthma, Cancer, Chronic Bronchitis, COPD

SKIN
Acne, Cancer, Dermatitis, Eczema, Wrinkles

BLOOD VESSELS
Atherosclerosis, Elevated Cholesterol and Triglycerides, High Blood Pressure, Hypertension, Varicose Veins

IMMUNE SYSTEM
Auto-Immune Disorders, Cancer, Crohn's Disease, Chronic Imflammation, Hepatitis, Herpes, HIV

BRAIN
ADHD, Alzheimer's, Austism, Bipolar Disorder, Cancer, Dementia, Depression, Insomnia, Lou Gherig's Disease (ALS), Migraines, Mood Swings, Multiple Sclerosis, Obsessive-Compulsive Disorder, Parkinson's

HEART
Angina, Arrhythmia, Congestive Heart Failure, Heart Attack, High Blood Pressure, Stroke

KIDNEYS
Chronic Kidney Disease, Renal Nephritis

ORGANS
Chronic Fatigue, Diabetes, Fibromyalgia, Irritable Bowl Syndrome, Heavy Metal Toxicity, Rapid Aging

JOINTS
Osteo-Arthritis, Psoriatic Arthritis, Rheumatoid Arthritis

Oxidative stress contributes to the emergence and worsening of many chronic diseases.

The image on the following page shows two PET scans of the brains of two different children. The one on the right is of a Romanian orphan who was institutionalized shortly after birth. The scan was done after the fall of its communist government in 1989, and shows the effects of extreme isolation and lack of nurturing, compared to a normal healthy child on the left. As you can see, the traumatized child has less overall brain activity, but especially in the temporal lobes (circled), which is integral for processing emotions and sensory inputs. This clearly illustrates the effect that prolonged stress has on your brain.

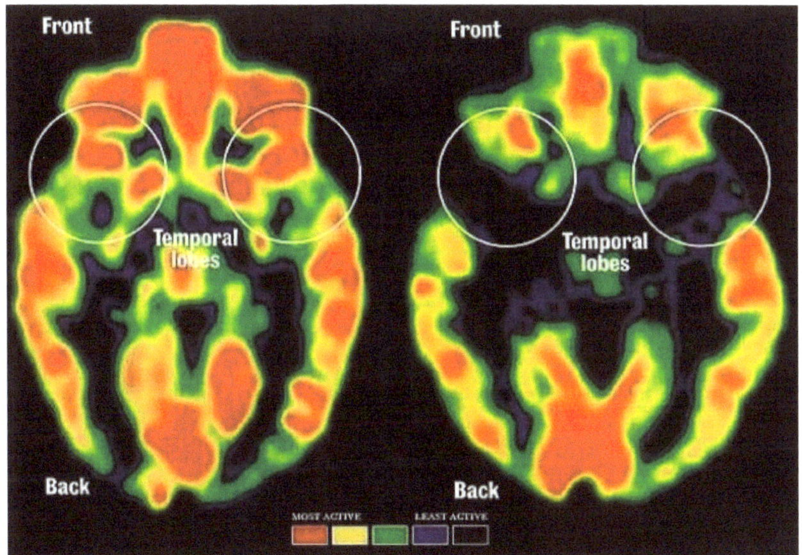

Two PET scans illustrating the effect that prolonged trauma has on early brain development. https://www.pnas.org/doi/10.1073/pnas.1911264116

We believe the good news is that with robust changes in lifestyle and personal attitude around the five integrated factors of spiritual purpose, family, community, exercise and nutrition, such damage can be repaired and these shortcomings can be overcome, or at least become a meaningful part of your life's mission turning them from scars into beauty marks.

Free radicals are also introduced to your body by your environment. Smoking and excessive drinking, pesticides like glyphosate on your food and pollutants in your water, industrial chemicals and cleaners, and excessive exposure to sunlight are all contributors to external sources of free radicals. In 2023, the United States Geological Survey (USGS) released a report that at least 45% of tap water in the United States is reported to be contaminated with "forever chemicals" like PFAS. This study tested for 32 of the over 12,000 known forever chemicals, so the actual prevalence is likely much more widespread. We *highly* recommend you invest in a reverse osmosis and home water softening system. It will benefit everything water touches in your home. Remember: you either filter your water, or you are the filter for what's in it.

Per- and Polyfluoroalkyl Substances (PFAS) in Select U.S. Tapwater Locations

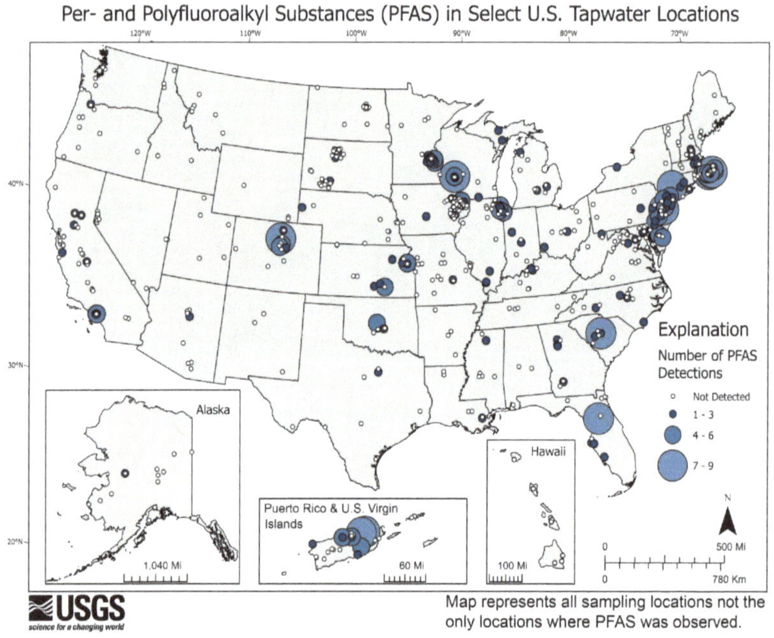

https://www.usgs.gov/news/national-news-release/
tap-water-study-detects-pfas-forever-chemicals-across-us

Antioxidants are the way we combat the harmful effect of free radicals on our life. They do this by allowing the free radical to absorb an electron without becoming a free radical themselves, or by breaking apart the free radical into constituent parts. Our body naturally produces antioxidants through hormonal regulation, enzymes produced in our cells and organs, body metabolism, and through genetic expression. Here are a few examples:

Our pineal gland produces melatonin, a hormone that makes us feel sleepy and also stimulates the production of antioxidative enzymes. This explains the common knowledge that adequate sleep is required for your body to repair itself.

Antioxidants are also produced through our body's metabolism. Uric acid is a significant antioxidant found in our blood's plasma. It is a byproduct of metabolizing purines, which are found in fermented alcohols, yeasts, shellfish, organ meats, and some types of fish. Biliruben (which makes our urine yellow) is another antioxidant produced when our body breaks down old red blood cells.

Our liver produces catalase, an enzyme that breaks down hydrogen peroxide (a free radical) into water and oxygen. Superoxide dismutase (SOD) is found in our cytoplasm, in our cell mitochondria, and in the spaces between cells. Coenzyme Q10 (available as a supplement called CoQ10) is one specific antioxidant found in cell mitochondria. Your DNA will actually instruct your cells to produce more antioxidants like CoQ10 during times of higher oxidative stress, but your ability to do so depends on lifestyle choices, such as your diet. The formation of these enzymes requires nutritional sources of zinc, copper and manganese (which are found in seeds, nuts, beans, whole grains, and other whole foods).

This is an important point: our bodies do not produce enough antioxidants on our own to sufficiently counter the effects of free radicals; hence the importance of obtaining them through our diet. Dietary supplements are not substitutions! Studies show that antioxidant supplements are less effective at combatting oxidative stress than diets rich in antioxidant foods.

The vast majority of antioxidants in our diet are found in the essential oils and other compounds of plants. While there are numerous vitamin supplements available, our body is better at absorbing nutrients from our food than from a pill. And who wants to eat pills for lunch anyway? Eating a mostly vegetarian diet of fresh organic foods will greatly increase the amount of antioxidants in your body, and help counter the damaging effects of free radicals.

POLYPHENOLS

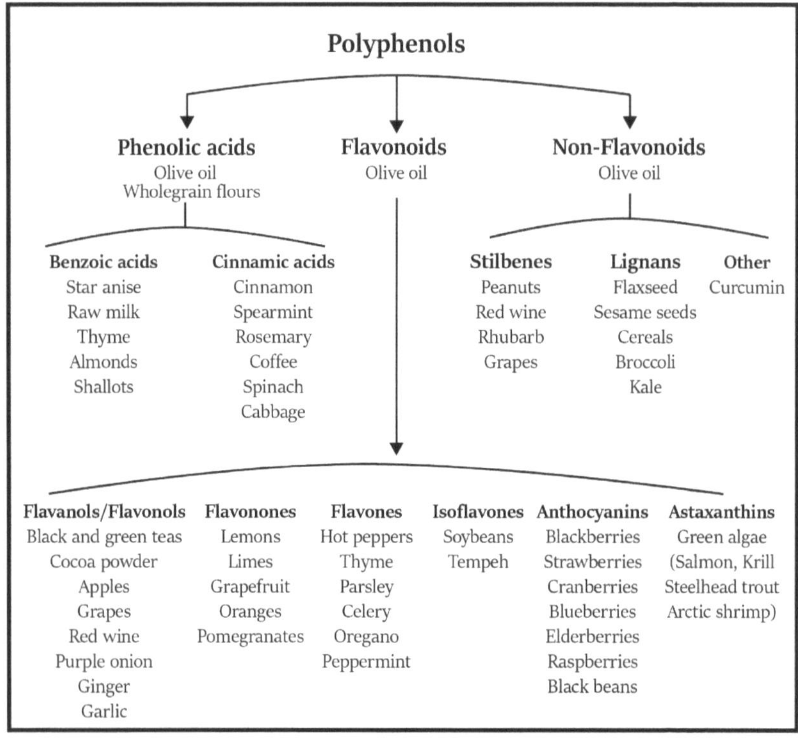

The major categories of polyphenols and some of the foods they
are found in.

Polyphenols are beneficial plant compounds with antioxidant
properties. There are thousands of different polyphenols, and many
of them are found in the skins and seeds of plants, contributing
to their vibrant and unique colors. These compounds help protect
the plant from diseases and predators, help it stay fresh, attract
pollinators, and contribute to its flavor. So they are most prevalent
when the plant is at its peak health and ripeness. Yet another reason
to buy your food at your local farmers market.

The above chart is of course by no means comprehensive, and
many plants contain a wide variety of polyphenols. All polyphenols

have anti-inflammatory properties, as they combat the effects of free radicals. Naturally occurring benzoic acids protect against fungal and bacterial infection, and help soothe skin irritation. Cinnamic acids help stimulate healthy gut flora, have been shown to protect the brain from Alzheimer's and dementia, improve blood glucose markers, reduce effects of gum disease, and help protect against sun burns and skin cancer. Stilbenes have demonstrably robust anti-cancer properties. Lignans help reduce the risk of heart disease, symptoms of menopause, osteoporosis, and breast cancer. Curcumin (found in black peppercorns) is a notable anti-inflammatory, especially when paired with turmeric.

Flavonoids as a category cover a huge range of plants, and boast a similarly huge range of health benefits. Flavonoids help lower high blood pressure and prevent blood clots from forming, improving blood flow around the body. This helps reduce inflammation around the body, from the nerve endings in your brain to the capillaries in your feet. Extra virgin olive oil is the go-to source for hundreds of polyphenol compounds. As it is an oil, many other plant essential oils are soluble in it, and it becomes a convenient way to enhance your foods with their beneficial flavors while delivering their health benefits.

There you have it. We have come full circle. We hope that you have learned some of the science and chemistry behind how and why you should incorporate infused olive oil into your diet, and pray that you will find purpose in your health and longevity to be moved by the spirit of God to do good works in this world.

CHAPTER 4

Sauces & Salsas

Much like a lyric soprano supported by an orchestra in a Mozart opera, the recipes in this chapter contain timeless sauces and salsas designed to feature olive oil with a supporting cast of all stars. Pesto, hummus, mayonnaise, chutney, and ajvar are just some of the classics in this chapter.

HUMMUS

It's easy to make delicious and creamy hummus at home without the preservatives, emulsifiers, and seed oils you typically find in store bought hummus. This recipe works well with our Rosemary Garlic or Lemon Basil infused oil, but you can also make unique blends with sage, thyme and oregano.

- 1/2 pound raw garbanzo beans
- 1 teaspoon baking soda
- 1/2 large white/yellow onion
- 1 large carrot
- 1 celery rib
- 10 garlic cloves, peeled and chopped
- 2 lemons, juiced
- 1 cup tahini
- Salt to taste
- 2-4 tablespoons infused olive oil

Soak your garbanzo beans overnight with the baking soda (this helps soften them). Rinse and add to a stock pot. Make a mirepoix (2:1:1 ratio of onion, carrot and celery) and add it to your chickpeas. You'll be removing the mirepoix later, so don't chop the pieces very small. Cover everything with water and cook it all on a simmer until the garbanzos are falling apart, about 2 hours.

In your blender, add the chopped garlic and enough fresh squeezed lemon juice to cover it. Let it sit for a few minutes. The citric acid from the juice will soften the bite of the garlic. Add your hot cooked chickpeas to your blender and 1 cup of the water they were cooked in. Blend at your lowest setting. If it becomes too thick, stop your blender and push down anything stuck on the side of the blender, and add slightly more cooking liquid. Continue until your texture is smooth and creamy with no grittiness. *Do not add olive oil to the blender.* The speed of the blades will slice the molecules of oil apart, releasing bitter flavors. Transfer to a mixing bowl and whisk in 1 cup of tahini paste. Salt to taste, and allow to cool before serving. When you're ready to serve, drizzle your favorite infused olive oil. There are plenty of great toppings to add, such as "everything" seasoning, powdered paprika and minced roasted red pepper, pine nuts, minced Kalamata olives, whole garbonzos, or pesto.

BABA GANOUSH

This traditionally Lebanese dip translates as "pampered daddy" (*baba*: an affectionate paternal nickname like daddy, and *ganoush*: spoiled or pampered). Infused flavors of thyme and oregano work well in this alternative to hummus, but also cumin and coriander, or rosemary.

- 2 pounds large eggplants
- 3 cloves garlic, peeled
- 1/4 cup tahini
- 1 lemon, juiced
- 1/4 cup infused olive oil
- Salt to taste

Pierce the eggplants with a paring knife, and stuff the slits with the garlic. Cook them over indirect heat in your smoker (preferred) or oven at 400^0 F until the eggplants are charred and completely deflated, about 45 minutes. They should be completely soft.

Scoop the insides and roasted garlic off the skins into a strainer, and discard the skins. Press the pulp lightly against the strainer to reduce the liquid as much as possible without losing any of the smoky roasted solids. A salad spinner also works. While it is draining, add the tahini to a large mixing bowl and squeeze the juice of one lemon into it. Whisk until integrated, and add the pulp. Mash it together with a fork while slowly adding the infused olive oil, one splash at a time, until all the ingredients are well mixed. Salt to taste.

Makes about 1 quart. Serve with pita bread, as a dip with julienned raw vegetables, or as a sandwich spread.

CILANTRO MINT CHUTNEY

Chutney originated in India, but has grown into a world wide and diverse condiment. At its core, it is a thicker blended sauce used for dipping or drizzling. From there, it can be fruited, savory, sweet, spicy or tart, or even a balanced mix of all these flavors. This chutney focuses on savory and spicy, and tastes great when drizzled over pan seared scallops, cod, halibut, or shrimp, but you can also add it to rice. Make this recipe in a mortar and pestle if you have forearms of steel and want a creamier consistency. Otherwise, you can use a blender.

- 1 bunch cilantro
- 1 small white onion
- 1 clove garlic
- 1 habanero or bird eye pepper (optional)
- 1/4 cup Mint Ginger infused olive oil

Finely mince together your cilantro, onion, garlic and hot pepper. Transfer everything to a mixing bowl and squeeze in the juice of one lemon. For the infused olive oil, spearmint has much less menthol than peppermint and balances better with the cilantro, but it's really a matter of taste. Add the Ginger Mint oil slowly and mix to emulsify. You want just enough oil that you have the consistency of a slurry rather than a paste. Makes 1 pint.

PESTO

A great sauce that is better made in a mortar and pestle than a blender, pesto has lots of subtle variations. Using fresh basil with the raw garlic will give your pesto a sharp, pungent, and spicy flavor that punches you in the nostrils. It's amazing. Cutting the basil with arugula is common, and this replaces some of the edge from basil with peppery and astringent flavors. The best parmesan is the one you just shaved off a block. Don't use that powdered stuff. Pine nuts are traditional, but considerably more expensive than walnuts.

- 2 cups of fresh picked basil, packed
- 1 cup of fresh arugula, packed
- 3 cloves garlic
- 2 tablespoons capers
- 1 tablespoon coarse sea salt
- 1/2 cup walnuts or pine nuts
- 1/4 cup shaved parmesan cheese (optional)
- 2 to 4 tablespoons Lemon Basil infused olive oil

Start by adding the garlic, capers, and salt to the mortar. Mashing and grinding these first ingredients helps them incorporate evenly when adding your leaves and nuts. Basil is hard to grind in a mortar, so it's easier if you first give your leaves a chop or two with your chef's knife. Adding the nuts at the same time as the leaves helps give the ingredients something to grind against. As you are mashing in the cheeese, add your infused olive oil one tablespoon at a time until you get the consistency you like. Makes about 1 quart.

HOMEMADE AIOLI

Aioli is a Spanish Mediterranean sauce that combines the words "ai" (garlic) and "òli" (oil, specifically olive oil). Today, in American cuisine it basically translates to garlic mayonnaise. Once you make fresh mayonnaise at home you'll never go back to that store bought, vegetable oil stuff! This results in a slightly-thinner-than-sandwich-spread aioli that is amazing when drizzled over fish, poached eggs, or asparagus. We use this aioli in our potato salad recipe.

- 1 farm fresh chicken egg
- 1/2 lemon, juiced
- 1 teaspoon stone ground mustard
- 1/2 teaspoon smoked paprika
- 1 cup Rosemary Garlic olive oil

Add all your ingredients to a 1/2 quart canning jar and allow the oil to float to the top. You want to use the whisk attachment on your immersion blender, and use it on the lowest speed setting. Don't use the blade attachment, because it will break the molecular strands of the olive oil, increasing the bitterness of the sauce. Place the whisk down in the very bottom of the jar and go. The emulsion should occur fairly quickly, so the longer you whisk the thicker it will get. After about 2 minutes it should barely drip off the whisk. For an herbed mayonnaise, consider oil infusions with thyme and sage, or dill. Makes 1 pint.

AJVAR

Ajvar is a Serbian side dish similar to hummus or baba ganoush but made with Ajvarski peppers, a mild, heart-shaped red pepper. These peppers develop a robust and unique flavor when grilled that is simply not possible to reproduce using a red bell pepper. Don't try this with red bell peppers. If you're like us and get blank stares when asking for real Ajvarski peppers at your farmers markets, you can buy organic and heirloom seeds from **RareSeeds.com** and grow your own.

- 2 pounds of Ajvarski peppers, seeded and roasted
- 1 large eggplant, roasted
- 2 tablespoons white vinegar
- 1/4 cup garlic infused olive oil
- Salt to taste

Poke slits in your eggplant to allow steam to escape and prevent explosions. Cut the peppers in half and remove the seeds. Roast the peppers and eggplant in a smoker or over indirect heat a charcoal grill at 400^0 F for about 15-20 minutes. The skins should be blackened and charred, and the eggplant should be deflated on itself and completely soft. Place them into a bowl to cover with a towel so they steam for a few minutes as they cool. This will help you scrape the flesh of the eggplant and peppers off their skins. Discard the skins. Add everything to a pot along with a splash or two of white vinegar, and blend it together with an immersion blender. Add your infused olive oil. Heat everything on a low simmer to evaporate the excess liquid and carmelize slightly. The finished sauce should be fairly smooth with a thick consistency.

SPICY TOMATO TAPENADE

Meathead Goldwin's website **AmazingRibs.com** has an excellent recipe for smoked cherry tomatoes. To make them, slice 1 pound of cherry tomatoes lengthwise and place them cut side up on an oven safe mat. Sprinkle with salt and dried basil, and smoke them for approximately 3 hours at 220^0 F (time will vary with ambient temperature). They are done when they have transformed into shriveled tomato raisins, and are absolutely bursting with smoky flavor. This is a great topping to add to salads, soups, and this spicy tomato tapenade.

- 2 cups smoked cherry tomatoes
- 1 teaspoon cumin seeds
- 1 teaspoon mustard seeds
- 2 teaspoons coriander seeds
- 1/2 teaspoon coarse sea salt
- 1 to 2 cloves of garlic
- 2 tablespoons of Hot Pepper infused olive oil

In a dry pan over medium heat, toast the seeds until lightly browned. Add them to your mortar with the salt and garlic, and mash with your pestle into a paste. Add two cups of smoked tomatoes and mash until everything is mostly incorporated. Add 2 tablespoons of hot chili infused olive oil, or more to taste.

OLIVE TAPENADE

Using a mortar and pestle to mash raw or toasted ingredients is an ancient way to produce robust and emulsified flavors in sauces. The result is creamier and with a richer flavor than what's possible from a blender. This tapenade can be served as an appetizer with whole grain crackers, smeared inside a fresh pita to accent a sandwich, or added to an omelet with wilted spinach and feta. Warning: do not sneak up and kiss your wife after eating this!

- 3 garlic cloves
- 1/3 cup capers
- 1 anchovy
- 1.5 pounds green olives
- 1 tablespoon oregano infused olive oil

You'll need a decent sized mortar and pestle, once that can hold about 4 cups. Add the garlic, capers, and anchovy, and mash until well blended. Drain 2 cans of your favorite green olives and slowly add these to your mortar, mashing away. Once everything has a creamy but chunky consistency, add one tablespoon of oregano infused olive oil, and mix gently. Makes about 2 quarts.

MARINARA SAUCE

There are, of course, at least a dozen flavor directions to take a marinara. Here we present one that has a lot of garden vegetables, but there's a reason tomato sauce is considered one of the five mother sauces. It's important to taste as you go, and build your sauce by adding the right ingredients at the right time to draw out the most flavor.

- 2 pounds of roma tomatoes, cored
- 1 large yellow onion, chopped
- 2-3 anchovies
- 5 garlic cloves, chopped
- 2 large carrots, chopped
- 2 ribs celery, chopped
- 1 quart low/no sodium chicken stock (or filtered water)
- 750ml dry red wine
- 1 cup basil leaves, packed
- 1 cup Rosemary Garlic infused olive oil
- 1 teaspoon coase sea salt, plus more to taste

Build your sauce by softening the onion over medium heat in a tablespoon or two of ghee or olive oil (this oil doesn't need to be infused because you won't be able to taste it after piling on the other ingredients), and then the anchovies and chopped garlic. You must use the anchovies. The finished sauce won't taste fishy, but imparts a subtle umami richness. Stir until the fish is dissolved, making sure the garlic softens but doesn't brown.

Add your tomatoes and sea salt. Some people don't like the skins, but in this recipe we leave them on both for their nutritional benefit, and later we will be blending the sauce in the pot grinds them up anyway. Cook them down until the skins start to fall off, about 10 minutes. At this point, you could leave your sauce as is, or rough chopped additional vegetables for a more robust garden flavor, such as: 3 large portobello mushroom caps, 1 medium zuchinni, and 1 green bell pepper.

Once your vegetables are softened, add your stock or water, and wine. We prefer robust flavors like a Grenache-Sangiovese blend, but you can do well with a Cabernet Sauvignon too. Pick what you think tastes good, but do not use a sweet wine. Once it starts to simmer, reduce the heat to low and let it reduce for 2-3 hours, stirring occasionally, until you have about 3 quarts left. Your sauce should be a rich and deep purple red. At this point you will add your basil leaves, and go to town with your immersion blender, making sure everything is nice and smooth. Taste to see if it needs more salt. Add several glugs of your favorite herb-infused olive oil, and simmer on low about 5 minutes or until the sauce starts to burp air bubbles. Taste it again to see if it needs more salt.

SMOKEY TOMATILLO SALSA

The smoky flavor in this salsa is a real crowd pleaser. Once everything is blended, add your infused hot pepper olive oil to your desired level of spiciness. Makes about 2 quarts.

- 1 pound tomatillos
- 1 large yellow onion
- 1/2 bunch cilantro
- 1 medium avocado
- 1 lime, juiced
- Hot Pepper infused olive oil, to taste
- 1 teaspoon sea salt

De-paper and rinse 1 pound of fresh tomatillos, then slice in half. Place them on a baking sheet (cut side up) along with a large yellow onion cut in quarters, and cook them in a pellet smoker at 325° F for 20 minutes. Hickory imparts a rich smoky flavor, which works better here than fruit woods. By the time they're done, the tomatillos should have turned a dull green, and everything should have charred a little bit. Add them to a blender with the lime juice, half a bunch of cilantro, a medium avocado, and salt.

CHAPTER 5

Vegetable Side Dishes

Eat a rainbow of nutrition by bringing the entire garden to the table. These vegetable sides typically compliment a bigger meal, but could also be paired together or with a meat, grains, or salad dish.

BRUSSELS SPROUTS

Brussels sprouts (like most vegetables) get a bad rap because too often they are served mushy and unseasoned. The key to making them taste great again is knowing how to cook and flavor them right.

- 1 pound brussels sprouts
- 3 strips of bacon
- Grated Parmesan to taste

- 1/4 cup of Rosemary Garlic infused olive oil
- 1 teapsoon of salt and pepper

Preheat your oven to 425° F. Wash your Brussels sprouts and trim off the stem end, then slice them in half from top to bottom. Spread them out evenly on a seasoned baking sheet, cut side down, and roast for 20 minutes. The high temperature ensures they get crispy and caramelized without getting mushy.

While they are cooking, dice up 3 strips of bacon. Add barely enough filtered water to your 8" skillet to cover the bottom (about 2-3 tablespoons), add your bacon, and cook on high until the water boils away, then reduce to medium-low and cover with a lid to prevent splatters. Parboiling the bacon this way ensures a more even rendering of the fat, so you don't end up with burnt meat and rubbery fat. Stir as needed, and allow to drain on a paper towel.

Remove the sprouts from the oven, and add to a mixing bowl with the bacon, Rosemary Garlic infused olive oil (or a flavor of your choice), salt and pepper, and toss to coat evenly. When plating, garnish with some finely grated Parmesan cheese.

ROASTED VEGGIES WITH BALSAMIC REDUCTION AND OLIVE OIL

Preheat your oven to 325^0 F and chop any of the following into nice bite sized pieces: bell pepper, broccoli florets, skinned sweet potato, parsnips, carrots, cauliflower, and radish. Spread evenly in a single layer on a baking sheet lined with parchment paper, sprinkle with salt and drizzle lightly with a balsamic vinegar. Bake until the root vegetables are fork soft, the florets are lightly singed, and the vinegar has mostly evaporated leaving behind a rich and sticky goo. About an hour, depending on how crowded your baking sheet is. Toss with a robust infused oil, such as rosemary and garlic, or thyme, oregano and basil.

BRUSCHETTA

We love "bruh-SKETTA" because it's a simple Italian appetizer with rich flavors. The key is choosing the freshest ingredients at peak ripeness. With that in mind, head down to your garden and farmers market in mid summer. Could you make it in January? Sure. Should you? Sure, just to taste the difference. Then, just... no.

- 1 head of garlic
- 8-10 basil leaves
- 1/2 shallot
- 1 tablespoon of red wine vinegar
- 5 tablespoons of Lemon Basil infused olive oil, divided
- 1 filone (the Italian version of a baguette)
- Kosher flaked salt for garnish

Slice a head of garlic just below the widest part of its diameter (but don't peel it), and roast it upside down in your oven at 350⁰ F for 30 minutes. While your garlic is roasting, dice your tomatoes into very small cubes. Mince the shallot so fine it almost looks like a paste. Stack the basil leaves and roll them like a little green cigar, slice them into delicate little strands, and add to the bowl. Add your red wine vinegar and Lemon Basil olive oil. Stir and let it sit.

Squeeze your now roasted garlic out of the skins into a small bowl and mash it up with a fork into a paste. Once that's done, heat your cast iron skillet over medium temperature, and slice your bread diagonally. Spread the roasted garlic on the top side, and toast the bottom side using butter, or a ghee infused olive oil. Remove the toast from the heat and spoon the tomato mix over it. Garnish with some flake salt.

MINI EGGPLANT PIZZAS

This is a fun little recipe that has no basis in any traditional Italian dish that we know of. Honestly, it's just something we came up with during the summer of 2020 as a way to try to incorporate more veggies while avoiding making a cauliflower "pizza" (because cauliflower smells like gym socks).

- 2 medium eggplants
- 1-2 cups Bruschetta (see previous page)
- 1/3 cup infused olive oil
- 1 ball of mozarella, sliced
- Chili flakes to taste

Peel a long eggplant in stripes, alternating between the purple skin and the pale flesh. Then slice it in circles about 1/2 inch thick. This gives a good texture and visual contrast without too much of the bitter skin. Dust with salt on both sides, and place on a paper towel. Once the water starts beading out of the top, mop it dry with another paper towel. You want to dry out your slices as much as possible to make room for the oil. Drizzle with Rosemary Garlic, Lemon Basil, or Hot Pepper infused olive oil and let it be absorbed.

If you like a little smoky flavor, set up your grill or smoker for indirect heat, at 325° F. Otherwise just place them on a glass baking dish. Cook the eggplant for 10 minutes and flip. It should be dried, not mushy. Spoon some bruschetta on it, then lay a 1/4" thick slice of fresh pulled mozzarella on top of that. Return to the oven. Once the cheese has melted, remove from the heat and garnish with your chili flakes, or basil strands.

STUFFED BELL PEPPERS

From a "ease of eating" standpoint, it's better to half your peppers lengthwise rather than cut off their tops. Scoop out the ribs and seeds, but leave the stem if you want that nice rustic look. There are so many options here for stuffing, basically anything can go in there. The key is to finely dice your ingredients, saute them, and finish everything under a broiler. Here is our standard garden mix:

- 2 medium eggplants
- 1 medium red onion
- 2 carrots
- 2 celery ribs
- 1 zuchinni
- 2 broccoli stems (not the florets)
- 1/4 cup Rosemary Garlic infused olive oil
- 1 ball of mozarella, sliced

Dice all your vegetables fairly small, such that several different pieces will be in each bite. Lightly salt, and saute on dry heat in a ceramic or cast iron skillet until softened. Turn off the heat and toss everything in an infused olive oil, such as Rosemary Garlic or a Mediterranean blend of oregano, thyme and sage. Optional: add just enough marinara sauce that everything mixes together. You don't want it to become watery. Top with some fresh mozarella and put it under your broiler for 30-60 seconds, or until the cheese starts to brown and bubble.

Some other stuffing ideas: cook and drain 1 pound of hamburger, then mix with rice and cilantro. Season with salt, infused olive oil, and cheese, then broil. Another option is to stuff with the Three Sisters Salad (page 70).

BLACK BEAN GARDEN MASH

This is a great way to clean out your fridge with leftover vegetables, and kids have no idea why it tastes so good! The veggies will dissolve their flavor and be overpowered by the beans, fresh herbs, and finishing olive oil, so it doesn't really matter what you add. Here's our standard:

- 1 pound of dry black beans
- 2 slices of bacon
- 1 medium onion
- Any non-spicy pepper (bell, poblano, etc.)
- 2-3 carrots
- 2-3 broccoli stems (not the florets)
- 1 squash (zuchinni, chayote, etc.)
- 1-2 large tomatoes
- 1-3 ribs of celery
- 4-7 radishes
- 4-5 garlic cloves
- 2 tablespoons oregano
- 2 tablespoons sage
- 2 tablespoons thyme
- 1/2 bunch cilantro
- 2 tablespoons cumin seeds
- Hot Pepper infused olive oil to taste
- Salt to taste

Rinse one pound of dry black beans and cover them with at least two inches of filtered water, a large pinch of salt, and one or two slices of bacon, diced. Bring this to a boil and then cover, letting it simmer until the beans are cooked, about two hours. Cooking your beans this way (instead of soaking and then tossing the water they soaked in) gives them a more rich flavor. While they are simmering, rough chop whatever leftover vegetables you have in your fridge and set aside.

Once the beans are ready, remove the lid and add your vegetables and cumin seeds and let it simmer uncovered. Once the carrots are soft enough to smoosh against the side of the pot with a spoon (about 15 minutes), add your fresh herbs, and let simmer another 5 minutes. You can use dried herbs if you don't want to pull the oregano and thyme off their stems. Using an immersion blender, grind up all the ingredients until well blended. Reduce heat to low and allow it to reduce to the thickness you like, stirring occasionally. Watch out for steam burps. Salt to taste once it's reached your desired consistency. Makes about 4 quarts.

You might have noticed I didn't add any hot peppers in earlier. Cooking them that long will reduce their spiciness to nothing. A recipe like this really likes a good hot pepper infused olive oil added at the end. We make ours with cayenne, allspice and roasted chicory.

SAUTEED GREENS (OR SAAG PANEER)

Saag Paneer is one of my favorite Indian dishes. Saag translates to "greens" and Paneer is a fresh cheese curd that doesn't melt, but does easily absorb spices. While many people associate this dish with spinach, its flavor is enriched by using greens in addition to spinach, such as arugula, chard, and kale (try to use just the leaves here. You can chop up the ribs and give them to your chickens). Together, these leafy greens add subtle peppery notes, and a diverse set of nutrients. To calculate how many greens you need, consider that each 10oz bag of leaves you add will reduce down to about 1.5 servings on a plate.

- 3lbs of baby spinach, chard, arugula and kale
- 1 medium white onion, diced
- 4 cloves garlic, minced
- 1 teaspoon cardamom seeds
- 1 tablespoon coriander seeds
- 1 cinnamon stick
- 1/2 pound paneer
- 1 cup of chicken stock (or water)
- 1/4 cup of Ginger Mint infused olive oil

Start with a large stock pot. Dice your onion and sauté it over medium heat in an unflavored olive oil until softened. Crush the cardamom with the side of your knife to crack open the pods to collect the black seeds. Add the minced garlic, cardamom seeds, cinnamon and coriander, and cook another minute or two. Take care the spices don't singe.

Add your greens one batch at a time and wilt them down. Once your greens are in, reduce your heat to low, and let them simmer for 45 minutes. Add splashes of chicken stock or filtered water as needed to prevent them from burning. About five minutes before finishing, remove the cinnamon stick and use an immersion blender to pulse blend a few times to loosely mix it together to your desired consistency. Aim for stems. Texture is good, but stringy is not. After you've blended it just right, fold in 8oz of paneer cut into cubes. Add the infused olive oil. Stir and serve hot.

GAZPACHO

This cold and raw soup puts forward rich flavors of tomato and olive oil, and is such a refreshing answer to a hot summer day! It originated in Spain in the Andalusian region.

- 1/2 pound paneer
- 2 pounds of tomatoes
- 1 large cucumber
- 1 green bell pepper
- 1 small shallot
- 2 slices of slightly stale bread
- 1 cup infused olive oil
- 2 splashes of red wine vinegar or sherry vinegar
- 2 tablespoons chives, minced
- Salt and pepper to taste

As with all tomatoes, the ones you want are those extra flavorful, thin-almost-translucent skinned, barely-holding-together bags of sun riped juice balloons from your farmers market. Smoosh them open with your hands into a mixing bowl, pull out the cores, and give them a thorough dusting of salt. Chop the following and add to your mixing bowl: one peeled and de-seeded cucumber, one de-seeded green bell pepper, and one small shallot. Add your vinegar. Let everything sit for half an hour so the salt and acid can extract the juices.

After the veggies have released their liquids somewhat, transfer everything to your blender, along with two slices of bread (slightly stale bread will absorb the juices better). Blend on low, and slowly add 1 cup of infused olive oil, such as Rosemary Garlic or Lemon Basil. For best results, blend until smooth, and strain out the leftover solids. Garnish with minced chives, cracked black pepper, and more olive oil.

STEAMED BROCCOLI

Suddenly, a very typical side of tiny edible trees now bursts with flavor!

- 1 lb. broccoli florets
- 3 tablespoons Lemon Basil olive oil
- Salt to taste

Cut the broccoli into florets and put in a steamer basket, saving your main stem for other recipes. Add a cup of filtered water and cover with a lid. Turn on high and bring to a boil. Remove the broccoli after it turns bright emerald green and before it turns dull. It should still have a slight crunch. Toss in a bowl with the oil and salt to coat evenly.

SAUTEED ASPARAGUS

For perfect asparagus that is neither mushy nor stringy, use a two stage cooking method of parboiling then sauteing.

- 1 pound asparagus
- 3 tablespoons of chicken stock (or filtered water)
- 1/2 lemon, juiced
- 2 tablespoons of Rosemary Garlic infused olive oil
- Salt and pepper to taste
- Optional garnishes

Put just enough water or chicken stock to barely cover the bottom of a 10" pan. Lay your trimmed asparagus all facing the same direction and turn the heat to high. They should not be fully submerged. Allow the liquid to braise the asparagus and evaporate fully. Once the liquid is boiled away, reduce the heat to medium and allow the dry heat to sear the asparagus. Get those grill marks! Once they start to stick, you can squeeze the juice of half a lemon on there, which helps deglaze the pan. Once they are done, dust with salt and pepper, then drizzle your Rosemary Garlic olive oil and shake the pan to roll them around in it.

Optional: garnish with fresh minced herbs like thyme and parsley, grilled lemon quarters, or diced bacon and grated Parmesan.

BROILED ZUCCHINI

Perfect for those giant summer zucchini your neighbor left on your doorstep!

- Zuchinni
- Salt
- Drizzles of Lemon Basil infused olive oil

Slice the zuchinni into half an inch thick discs. The more surface area the better. Dust with salt on both sides and let it rest for 10 minutes on a paper towel to draw out the moisture. Once you see beads of water on the top, pat it dry with a paper towel and place the slices on a cookie sheet, making sure not to overlap. Drizzle liberally with Lemon Basil olive oil and put under your broiler, near the top rack. Let it broil until nicely charred.

SWEET CARROTS

This makes a nice side, and brings a fresh fall flavor to the dinner table.

- 1/2 pound baby carrots
- 1/4 cup Ginger Mint infused olive oil
- 1/3 cup raw honey
- 1/2 tablespoon cinnamon powder
- 1/2 cup chopped pecans

Add everything to a small pot except the nuts and stir to mix. Cook on medium-low heat until the carrots are soft. Garnish with the chopped pecans. You can toast the pecans beforehand on dry heat for a little more crunch.

STUFFED POTATO SKINS

Perfect for game day, back-yard BBQ, or a family reunion, these stuffed potato skins substitute a few different ingredients to make them a little healthier. A great way to enjoy the Black Bean Garden Mash for dipping!

- 6 medium Russet potatoes
- 1 cup 5% fat Fage yogurt
- 3 strips of bacon
- 1/3 cup of multi-color bell peppers
- 1/4 cup yellow onion
- 1 green onion
- 1 cup shredded cheddar cheese
- 1/3 cup Rosemary Garlic infused olive oil
- Hot Pepper infused olive oil (optional, to taste)
- Salt and pepper to taste

Wash the potatoes clean from any dirt, and poke a few holes in them to allow steam to escape. Bake at 400° F until cooked fully through, about 1 hour. Remove them from your oven and while they are cooling, finely dice your bell peppers and onions and set aside. To cook your bacon, add just enough water to your saute pan to barely cover the bottom and parboil your bacon on high heat until the water evaporates, then turn the heat to low and cook until browned. This results in a more even rendering of the fat. Dice when finished.

Once the potatoes are cool, cut them in half lengthwise, and scoop out the insides, leaving a little next to the skin for stability. Mix the potato with the yogurt, infused olive oil, peppers and yellow onion, and bacon. Taste and add your salt and pepper.

Put the skins in an air fryer and cook at 400° F for 20 minutes, or until crisped. You can cook in a regular oven too, but it won't be as crispy. Add your filling, and top with chedder cheese. Put it under the broiler or back into the air fryer until the cheese melts and starts to bubble.

HASSELBACK SWEET POTATOES

When it's time to impress your dinner guests, you bake your potatoes Hasselback style.

- 4 similarly sized sweet potatoes
- 2 tablespoons of Spiced Orange infused olive oil, divided
- Pinch of salt
- 1/4 of chopped pecans

Since most potatoes don't have a flat side, the first thing to do is slice a thin amount off the flattest side to create one. Then nestle the potato lengthwise between two disposable chopsticks. Make evenly spaced cuts about 1/4" wide along the potato, using the chopsticks as guardrails to prevent you from accidentally slicing all the way through. Drizzle 1 tablespoon of your infused olive oil, sprinkle with salt and/or pepper as desired, and bake for 30 minutes at 400^0 F. Take them out of the oven, drizzle another tablespoon of infused olive oil into the separating slices, and bake for another 30 minutes. There are many options here for garnishing. Sweet potatoes love pecans

For baking potatoes consider Rosemary Garlic infused olive oil, and garnishings such as cheese, chopped bacon, or minced chives.

WEEKNIGHT GREEN BEANS

Sure, you could use fresh green beans or tomatoes, but this recipe was designed with the hurried parent on a budget in mind. To be as fast and simple as possible, we're breaking the mold of our own book in order to demonstrate that simple food can taste good even when it isn't plucked from a garden and delicately prepared.

- 1 pound frozen French cut green beans
- 12oz can of diced tomatoes
- 1/2 yellow onion, diced
- Salt and pepper to taste
- 2-3 glugs of Lemon Basil olive oil

Open the can of tomatoes and bag of green beans, and unceremoniously dump them in your cast iron skillet. Turn it up to medium heat, and while it's thawing, dice a small onion and throw that in there too. Stir to mix evenly. Give it a couple turns of the salt and pepper grinders. Once it's bubbling hot, turn off the heat and add two or three glugs of Lemon Basil infused olive oil. Simple and stunning side dish.

Salads

Ahh the salad... so much more than just leaves. Here are some classics from across the spectrum of ingredients such as fruit, pasta, potatoes, vegetables, cheese, or herbs, mixed together with a simple dressing.

CAPRESE

With such a simple salad, you can't settle for anything but the freshest ingredients. The very best caprese is made with basil picked right out of your summer garden, a tomato so ripe it's skin is about to burst, and fresh pulled mozzarella.

- 5 or 6 leaves of fresh basil
- 2 very ripe heirloom tomatoes
- 1 ball of fresh pulled mozzarella

- Drizzles of Lemon Basil infused olive oil
- Salt and cracked pepper

Cut your tomatoes and mozzarella into slices about 1/2" thick, and layer them on your plate. Rip or slice your basil leaves, and place them artfully around your plate. Drizzle liberally with your favorite infused olive oil, and fresh cracked salt and pepper. Lemon Basil olive oil works well here, or a blend of Mediterranean flavors like oregano, sage and thyme. Encourage the liquid from the tomatoes and cheese to fraternize with the oil to make a simple dressing.

CUCUMBER SALAD

At its most basic, the cucumber salad is made with cucumber, onion and tomatoes. From this starting point, there are so many delicious varieties to make. We will tell you what we like, and then offer a few different ways to direct the flavor.

- 2 English cucmbers
- 1/3 cup purple onion, diced
- 2 handfuls of cherry tomatoes
- 1 cup Kalamata olives
- 1/2 lemon, zested and juiced
- 2 tablespoons unfiltered apple cider vinegar
- 3oz feta cheese
- 1/3 cup Lemon Basil infused olive oil
- Salt and pepper to taste

Dice the cucumber and onion, and slice the olives and cherry tomatoes in half. Add it all to a mixing bowl, dust with salt and pepper, then the zest of the lemon. In a small bowl, stir together the lemon juice, olive oil, and vinegar, and pour it over the salad before it separates. Try to find a feta that comes in brine, rather than a pre-crumbled one. Chop or crumble it yourself, and gently fold it all together. The more you stir, the more the cheese will dissolve into the dressing so take care not to overdo it.

For variations on this theme: bell peppers are lovely when diced for a pop of color. Try mincing up some fresh cilantro or mint. The key is to not overload the number of ingredients, colors and flavors. Pick 4 or 5 and stick with that.

This salad is a great addition to lunch or dinner, either as a side dish or appetizer.

PASTA SALAD

Don't like cucumbers? Want more carbs to recover from your exercise routine? Swap out cucumbers for pasta as your base ingredient, and bam! Pasta salad. Everything in the last recipe makes a delicious pasta salad served cold. But there are other salads too:

- 1 pound orzo pasta
- 1/2 cup of hot pasta water
- 12oz can of artichoke hearts, diced
- 1 cup smoked cherry tomatoes
- 2 tablespoons parlsey
- 2 tablespoons oregano
- 1/3 cup of capers
- 1 cup green olives
- 1/3 cup Rosemary Garlic infused olive oil
- 1/3 cup grated Parmesan cheese
- 1 teaspoon fine ground black pepper

Bring a 4 quarts of water to a boil and add a tablespoon of salt and your orzo. We like orzo pasta because it's small and cooks quickly (6 minutes), and the grains will clump together more easily, allowing the flavors of the dressing to stay with it. While it's cooking, add your artichokes, tomatoes, capers and olives to a large mixing bowl. Mince your oregano and parsely, and add them to a small bowl, along with your herbs, olive oil, pepper and cheese. Drain the pasta, reserving 1/2 cup of starchy liquid. Add the pasta to the big bowl. Add the starchy water to the small bowl, and whisk vigorously until the cheese is melted and the sauce is emulsified. Toss the pasta with the dressing.

FRUIT SALAD

We were once sternly told at a farmers market that watermelon is God's favorite fruit, and nothing can make it better. But when they tasted some with Ginger Mint olive oil drizzled on it, they had to admit that even watermelon can be improved on. To make it the best way, your watermelon should be ice cold, and cubed on a plate swirled with oil.

But if you're looking to impress your friends with a fruit salad at your summer barbeque, use a melon baller to hollow out half a large watermelon and half a honeydew. Mix evenly together with blueberries and raspberries. Drizzle with Ginger Mint or a Spiced Orange infused oil just before serving.

COLESLAW

Coleslaw originated in The Netherlands as "koolsla", which means "cabbage salad", but is now widely loved as a southern barbeque side shared among families and friends. Here's our recipe for a large get together:

- 1 medium green cabbage
- 1 small purple cabbage
- 1/2 pound shredded carrot
- 1/2 cup of thinly sliced purple onion
- 1 red bell pepper
- 1/3 cup unfiltered apple cider vinegar
- 1/4 cup of Rosemary Garlic infused olive oil
- 2 tablespoons of honey
- 1 tablespoon of salt
- 1/2 tablespoon fine ground black pepper

Shred your cabbages, dice your bell pepper, and mix well with the carrot, onion and salt. Let it sit for 5 minutes to let the salt soften the vegetables. Mix the vinegar, olive oil, honey, and black pepper. Toss everything together to combine.

If you like a creamy coleslaw you can substitute the infused olive oil with the homemade aioli (page 30).

TABOULI

Tabouli, also spelled "tabbouleh," is derived from the Arabic word "taabil," meaning "seasoning" or "to spice." In this adaptation, we substitute our Ginger Mint infused olive oil for the fresh mint. It makes for a refreshing summer side salad with some falafel or a gyro sandwich.

- 1 cup of #1 bulgur
- 3 bunches of curley parsley
- 1/2 English cucumber
- 1 large tomato
- 2 green onion stalks
- 2 lemons, juiced
- 1/3 cup of Ginger Mint infused olive oil

Bulgur is an ancient whole grain rich in fiber and antioxidants. Pour 2 cups of boiling water over the bulgur and let it soak for an hour. Finely dice the cucumber and tomato. Season with salt and set aside, to allow the excess water to draw out. De-stem the parsley (you can save the stems for black bean mash on page 44) and add to a food processor, along with the green onions and lemon juice. Pulse blend until well minced. Drain the water that has seeped out of the cucumber and tomato (you can freeze this in an ice cube tray to add a shot of electrolytes to your water after working outside). Drain your bulgur and combine all the ingredients with the infused olive oil.

FRIED APPLE KALE SALAD

A fruit forward salad pairs very well with a fruit forward infused olive oil, such as Spiced Orange (orange peel, cinnamon, ginger, allspice and clove). Use a denser apple like Fuji or Granny Smith.

- 8 kale leaves, de-ribbed
- 1 small apple
- 1/4 cup of Spiced Orange infused olive oil
- 1 handful of dried cranberries
- 1 small handful of sliced almonds

Rough chop your kale into bite sized pieces. Core your apple and slice thinly, about 1/4" thick, and sprinkle with a pinch of salt. Wait 5 minutes for them to sweat, and pat the slices dry. Heat your pan until droplets of water evaporate immediately, then add the apples in a single layer to the dry pan. After 30 seconds, flip the apples and add the oil. Turn off the heat and add the kale, flipping it and stirring it until it softens in the residual heat. Plate the kale and apples, and garnish with sliced almonds and dried cranberries.

STRAWBERRY FIELDS SALAD

"Spring mix" (a mix of about 15 different leaves including spinach, arugala, chard, baby kale, different red and green lettuces, mizuna, and cabbage) makes the base for this salad. This mix is marketed as "spring mix" and sold in most grocery stores. Whether you buy it pre-packaged or grow it in your garden, the bitterness of these greens is offset by a fruit-forward infused olive oil such as a Spiced Orange, or a menthol-forward Mint Ginger.

- 1 plate of spring mix
- 3 strawberries, sliced
- 1 or 2 purple onion slices
- 1/4 cup of chopped pecans
- 1-2oz of soft goat cheese

Mix the oil in a large bowl with a pinch of salt and a splash of apple cider vinegar. Add your mix and toss to coat evenly.

Top your salad with sliced strawberries, paper thin slices of purple onion, pecans, and a nice goat cheese.

DECONSTRUCTED SPRING ROLL SALAD

This salad blends Thai and Vietnamese flavors with classic spring roll ingredients for a family favorite. There are a lot of flavors going on here, nonetheless, it is possible to have infusions shine through by adding spicy infused oil to the peanut sauce and ginger mint infused oil to the chicken and noodles.

- 2 heads of romaine lettuce, chopped
- 1/3 cup of basil, chopped
- 1 cup of shredded carrots
- 2 green onion stalks, sliced
- 1 cup of purple cabbage, shredded
- 2 avocados, diced
- 1 mango, diced
- 1 English cucumber, sliced
- 1/2 pound of flat glass noodles
- 3 chicken thighs
- 3/4 cup of no-sugar added peanut butter
- 1/4 cup low sodium soy sauce
- 1/4 rice vinegar
- 1 lime, juiced
- 2 tablespoons of raw honey
- 4 dashes of toasted sesame oil
- Hot Pepper infused olive oil to taste
- 1/2 cup of Ginger Mint olive oil, divided
- 1/3 cup of crushed peanuts

Cube up the chicken thighs and dust with salt, then add to a hot pan with 1/4 cup of Ginger Mint olive oil. Cook covered over heat low enough that the chicken cooks through but doesn't brown. Set aside and allow to cool. In a new pot, heat 4 quarts of water to a boil and cook your noodles. Drain and cool, then toss with 1/4 cup of Ginger Mint olive oil.

For the salad, combine the romaine, carrots, green onions, mango, cilantro, and cucumber in a large mixing bowl.

For the dressing, whisk together the no-sugar added peanut butter, low sodium soy sauce, rice vinegar, lime juice, raw honey, toasted sesame oil, and 1-3 tablespoons of Hot Pepper infused olive oil to your desired level of heat. This can be made ahead of time and refrigerated.

Mix the noodles, salad ingredients, and dressing together thoroughly. Garnish with crushed peanuts.

POTATO SALAD

This salad uses the Rosemary Garlic Aioli dressing recipe (page 30). The parsley makes for a nice winter potato salad. For a summer version, substitute with 3-4 sprigs of tarragon.

- 6 yellow potatoes
- 2 green onion stalks
- 1/3 purple onion, diced
- 1/4 bunch of curly parsley
- 2/3 cup of Homemade Aioli
- Salt and pepper to taste

Cut the potatoes into bite sized pieces (about 1 inch cubes) and simmer them until soft. While they are cooking, slice the green onions diagonally, dice up the purple onion, and add them to a mixing bowl. Add the aioli, and toss to coat and distribute all the ingredients evenly. You have added enough when the dressing lightly coats the ingredients.

THREE SISTERS SALAD

Beans, corn and squash are called the three sisters in Native American agriculture because they have a symbiotic relationship in the garden. Beans are nitrogen fixing, which helps the corn. The corn provides a natural trellis for the squash to vine up. The leaves of the squash provide shade to the bean plants and the soil. Together, they provide carbs, protein, fiber, and amino acids. Whether you're farming your own or buying from a store, it only takes a few simple ingredients to make this salad.

- 2 chayote squash (or 1 zuchinni)
- 1 ear of corn, cut off the cob
- 1 cup of black beans
- 1/4 cup of cilantro, minced
- 1 lime, juiced
- Salt to taste
- 1/4 cup of infused olive oil

Dice the squash and cut the corn off the cob. We like to toast everything over dry heat until the squash starts to brown and the corn starts to pop. Remove from the heat and add to a bowl with the cooked black beans and cilantro. For the dressing, combine 1/4 cup of infused olive oil, such as cumin and lime peel, or our Rosemary Garlic with lime juice, and a pinch or two of salt.

CHAPTER 7

Fish, Meat & Eggs

Despite the old wive's tale, you can sauté with olive oil. But it is preferable from a flavor perspective to apply oil afterward, absorb the oil into the fat, or cook quickly. Here are a few ways to work around the evaporation of tasty aromas with lamb, steak, eggs, fish and chicken.

SOUS VIDE LAMB CHOPS

Sous vide is a more precise way to reverse sear your chops, and it allows you to baste your meat in flavors longer than you could in a cast iron skillet. This method works best with well marbled cuts, because the intramuscular  fat will render and intermingle with the infused oil flavors. It also works for ribeye steaks.

- 4 lamb chops
- 1/3 cup Rosemary Garlic infused olive oil

- 1 teaspoon of salt

Start by freezing an ice cube of infused olive oil in a silicone ice cube tray. Rosemary and garlic infused oil make classic lamb flavors that work very well here. If you're feeling adventurous try Ginger Mint infused oil. If you are poaching 2 lamb chops in a bag use approximately a frozen 1/4 cup cube, if you are poaching 4 in a bag use approximately a frozen 1/3 cup cube. It's fine not to be exactly precise here; the point is moderation. If you're cooking more than 4 lamb chops, prep another bag. Lightly salt your lamb chops and add the frozen olive oil cube. Cook to perfect rare at 125^0 F for 3 hours, or if you must, medium rare at 130^0 F.

When the chops are done, remove them from the bag and pat them dry on a paper towel. Discard the liquid. You can refrigerate the cooked chops at this point in an airtight container to eat later, or you can give them a proper sear on your screamin' hot cast iron skillet with a little unflavored olive oil or butter. To ensure a great sear make sure the skillet is very hot, flip the meat frequently, and baste continuously.

DEVILED EGGS

The secret to easy peel boiled eggs is not overcooking them, and rapidly cooling them down once they're finished. Here we present a classic deviled egg recipe that's perfect for a pot-luck, but feel free to experiment  with more exotic and delicately placed toppings if you're planning a more intimate dinner setting, such as caviar, dill fronds, minced chives, or marmalade.

- 1 dozen eggs
- 1 cup infused aioli
- Garnish with cayenne powder

You'll get a perfectly firm yolk if you add your eggs to already boiling water and cook for 12 minutes. Transfer to a large bowl of ice water, running more cold water over it while you mix them around to cool off.

Once they are cool enough to handle, tap the end and roll it along your counter, pressing gently to crack the shell so it peels off. Slice in half lengthwise, and pop the yolk into a mixing bowl. Add the aioli sauce (page 30) and mash everything together into a thick paste with a wooden spoon. Scoop the mixture into a gallon refrigerator bag and snip off a corner. Pipe the mix through into the hollow part of the egg white and garnish with a sprinkle of cayenne powder.

GRILLED CHEESE SANDWICH

Toasting your bread with Rosemary Garlic olive oil allows the flavors to be absorbed and presented as the first point of contact with your taste buds. You need about 1 tablespoon of oil per slice of bread. Preheat your pan to medium heat prior to dropping in your oil, and put your bread on it immediately. Tilt the pan around to make sure it coats evenly and soaks in. (Pro tip: this also works great when toasting buns for hamburgers!) Add your cheese at the same time as your bread, and cover with a lid to trap the heat and melt the cheese faster.

So many options here for a good grilled sammich! Cheddar, bacon and tomato? Brie and prosciutto? Basil leaf and mozzarella?

CHICKEN CREPES ON A BED OF SPINACH

This meal makes a fancy Friday night dinner or Sunday brunch, and is relatively fast if you make the chicken and yogurt sauce ahead of time.

For the chicken:

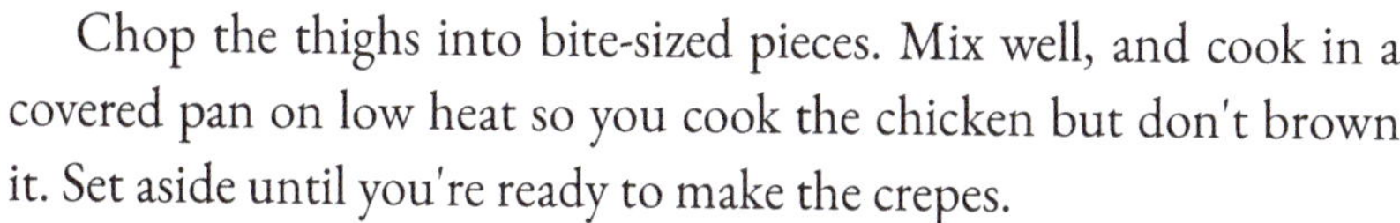

- 4 boneless skinless chicken thighs
- 1/2 lemon zest
- Generous pinch of salt
- 1/4 cup of Rosemary Garlic infused olive oil

Chop the thighs into bite-sized pieces. Mix well, and cook in a covered pan on low heat so you cook the chicken but don't brown it. Set aside until you're ready to make the crepes.

For the yogurt sauce:

- 1 large cucumber
- 1 cup of 5% fat Fage yogurt
- 2 sprigs of mint leaves
- 1/2 lemon juice
- Small pinch of salt

Skin the cucumber, slice it lengthwise, and scoop out the seeds. Add everything to a blender, and blend until smooth and set aside. Fage is preferred because it has no added sugar.

For the bed of spinach:

- 8oz of spinach per plate
- 1/4 cup of purple onion per plate
- 1/4 cup of Rosemary Garlic infused olive oil

Dice the onion, and soften it over medium heat without any oil. Lightly chop the spinach to minimize stringiness. Once it is wilted down, add the infused olive oil and turn off the heat (or lower to barely warm) and add 1 spoonful of your yogurt sauce per plate. Stir to incorporate. Keep your spinach warm while preparing the crepes.

For the crepes:

- 2 farm fresh eggs
- 1 cup all purpose flour
- 1.5 cups of whole milk
- 1 tablespoon of melted butter
- 1/2 tablespoon of Rosemary Garlic infused olive oil per crepe

Add everything to a blender except the oil and blend until foamy; allow it to settle. Heat your cast iron on medium until it is hot but not smoking hot, and add just a splash of Rosemary Garlic olive oil. Scoop 1/2 cup of crepe batter onto the pan and immediately tilt the pan around to spread it out. Cook until it is dry on the surface and flip, cooking another few seconds. It's better to cook all your crepes first before stuffing/rolling them.

Plate your spinach first, then add a thin line of yogurt sauce and a layer of chicken, and roll the crepe like an enchilada. Top them off with another dollop of yogurt sauce.

GRILLED TROUT WITH LEMON CAPER SAUCE

The humble lemon and caper sauce first originated in the coastal Mediterranean in ancient times. French cuisine later added additional flavor complexities such as herbs and wine.

- 2 Rainbow Trout fillets
- Salt to taste
- 3 tablespoons of Lemon Basil infused olive oil
- 1 tablespoon ghee infused olive oil (or unsalted butter)
- 3oz Pinot Grigio
- 1 lemon, juiced
- 1 sprig of fresh thyme
- 2 tablespoons of capers

To reduce splatter, dust your filets with salt and rest them on a paper towel for 10 minutes, then pat them dry. Heat your skillet over medium flame and add three tablespoons of Lemon Basil infused olive oil. Once it starts to shimmer, lay your filets skin side down, add your thyme and capers. As the edges of the fish skin starts to brown, tilt the pan slightly to pool the oil and spoon it over the fish. Continue until it is cooked and the skin starts to flake when pressed gently with a fork, about 4-5 minutes. Remove from the pan and let rest on a plate skin side up, so it doesn't get soggy.

Reduce your heat to low and deglaze the pan with a healthy splash of Pinot Grigio, then add the juice of a lemon, and add the ghee infused oil or unsalted butter. Whisk gently to emulsify and allow to reduce and thicken (about 5 minutes).

Plate your fish for serving skin side down, and drizzle the sauce over your fish. Delicious when served with wild rice and a side of steamed broccoli (tossed in Lemon Basil olive oil, of course).

BRAISED SALMON SOUP

This delightful one-pot soup incorporates lots of bright summer flavors, and is a fusion twist on a classic French soup.

- 2 salmon fillets (skin off)
- 1 small yellow onion
- 2 large carrots
- 1 small zucchini
- 1 small fennel bulb
- 2 cloves of garlic
- 1 thumb of ginger root
- 5 cherry tomatoes
- 1 sprig of tarragon
- 3 tablespoons Lemon Basil infused olive oil
- 2 cups chicken stock
- 2 cups of Sauvignon Blanc

Dice the onion, carrots and fennel, and saute in a large pan with unflavored olive oil until softened. Next, mince the garlic and ginger root, dice the zucchini, and add them to your pan. Saute for another minute, then add equal parts of chicken broth and Sauvignon Blanc. We recommend finding one with bright acidity and a good minerality to its finish, such as Sea Pearl from New Zealand. The goal is to fill the pan so that the vegetables are barely covered in liquid. Bring to a simmer. Rest your skinless salmon fillets on top of this and cover with a lid, so they are cooked from both directions by the soup broth below and by the steam above. Half inch thick fillets will cook in about 5 minutes. 1 inch thick fillets will cook in about 9 minutes. A thermometer should read 125° F.

In each serving bowl, mix together equal portions of halved cherry tomatoes, tarragon, and Lemon Basil olive oil, with a pinch of salt. Once the salmon is cooked, ladel the vegetables and broth over this, and then lay your salmon on top.

PERFECT BREAKFAST SCRAMBLE

Who doesn't love a good breakfast scramble? Of course, there are a million different variations but they all follow a similar method. Your pan is hot enough once flicking a drop of water on it causes the water to bounce around and then evaporate. Your eggs will be less likely to stick it's this hot, because it's hot enough to create a steam barrier between your eggs and the pan.

- 2 farm fresh eggs
- 1/3 cup of zucchini, diced
- 1/4 cup of purple onion, diced
- 1 handful of spinach, chopped
- 2oz soft goat cheese
- Salt to taste
- 2 tablespoons Rosemary Garlic infused olive oil

It's preferred to toast the zucchini and onion on a dry heat, as this prevents them from getting mushy. Once browned to your liking, add your spinach leaves and reduce the heat to low. Once the spinach is about halfway wilted, add 2-3 glugs of your favorite infused olive oil. We recommend our Lemon Basil or Rosemary Garlic, but a blend of thyme, oregano and sage works too. Immediately add your eggs, and stir constantly. By the time they are 75% cooked your spinach should be entirely wilted. Turn off the heat to your pan and add your cheese if desired. The residual heat from the pan will finish cooking the eggs and melt your cheese.

Serve with a side of fresh fruit, or toast with pesto or homemade jam.

STUFFED FRENCH TOAST

Despite its name, french toast is no more French than french fries. But speaks the language of delicious, which is good enough for our bellies! Brioche, Challa or Texas Toast does well because it absorbs the egg without falling apart, especially once it is slightly stale.

- 4 large farm fresh eggs
- 8 thick slices of brioche bread
- 1 cup of cream cheese, softened
- 1oz. Grand Marnier (optional)
- 1 teaspoon of pure vanilla extract
- 1 cup of whole milk
- 1/2 teaspoon of salt
- Powdered sugar for dusting
- Butter for sauteing
- 1/4 cup of Spiced Orange infused olive oil
- 2 cups of frozen berries
- Fresh berries for garnish
- Mint sprig for garnish

In a sauce pot, heat the frozen berries on medium until bubbling, then lower the heat and allow to reduce and thicken, about 20 minutes. Stir occasionally to make sure it doesn't burn. Prepare the cream cheese by whipping it with the vanilla and Grand Marnier until well incorporated, and set aside. Once the berry compote is reduced and thickened, add the infused olive oil.

In a larger mixing bowl, vigorously whisk together the milk, eggs and salt. Use a table knife to spread a liberal amount of cream cheese on a slice of bread, then lightly press another slice on top, making a cream cheese sandwich. Prepare all eight slices this way. Heat a pan on your stove. Soak the stuffed bread in the batter for 10-15 seconds, so it is well saturated, add your butter to the pan, and saute until each side is golden brown.

Sift the powdered sugar, drizzle several spoonfuls of berry compote, and garnish with the fresh berries and mint.

CHAPTER 8

Snacks & Desserts

Oh my goodness, has all this healthiness gotten in the way of having fun? Let's make some recipes that still use amazing olive oils but are at least feeding that sweet tooth a little.

MOVIE NIGHT POPCORN

For the best movie night popcorn, simply put a 1/2 cup of kernels into your air popper. Once finished, drizzle up to 3 tablespoons of Rosemary Garlic infused olive oil. If you like it spicy, substitute 1 tablespoon of Hot Pepper infused olive oil. But you could also use ghee infused olive oil if you truly want that butter flavor. Grind a little sea salt over it and you're ready to go. Make sure you already have your movie picked out, because your popcorn will be so delicious that everyone will eat it during the previews.

SOURDOUGH BREAD PUDDING

The caveat for this recipe assumes that you actually have left-over sourdough bread. What's more likely is you made some just for this recipe.

- 1 lb loaf of sourdough
- 2 farm fresh eggs
- 3 cups of whole milk
- 1 cup of golden raisins
- 1 cup of brown raisins
- 1/3 cup of Spiced Orange infused olive oil
- 1/2 cup of bourbon (optional)

Cut up your bread into 1″ cubes and measure out enough to fill up a glass baking dish. In a mixing bowl blend together your milk, spiced orange infused olive oil and farm fresh eggs. You can soak the raisins in the bourbon for 20 minutes if you like the flavor (the alcohol will evaporate during cooking), or just add them straight into your wet ingredients. Once it's all mixed, add your cubed bread and fold gently so that the bread soaks up the liquid without crumbling. Transfer everything to your baking dish and cook at 325^0 F until a toothpick comes out clean (about 20 minutes).

LEMON BASIL SUGAR COOKIES

The humble sugar cookie is elevated to new heights of grand-child-induced awe when you flavor them this way.

- 2-1/4 cups all purpose flour
- 1/2 teaspoon baking powder
- 1/2 teaspoon baking soda
- 1/2 teaspoon salt
- 1 lemon, zested
- 1-1/2 tablespoon dried basil
- 3 tablespoon coarse sugar
- 1/2 lemon, juice
- 1-1/4 cups of granulated sugar
- 1/3 cup of Lemon Basil infused olive oil
- 2 farm fresh eggs
- 1/2 teaspoon vanilla extract

Prepare a small bowl with equal parts lemon zest, dried basil (it works better here than fresh), and coarse sugar. Mix it thoroughly, allowing the oils from the zest to dampen the basil just slightly. Set aside for later.

Preheat your oven to 350⁰ F and line two cookie sheets with parchment paper. Sift together your dry ingredients into a large mixing bowl: flour (Cup4Cup makes a good gluten free alternative flour), baking powder, baking soda, and salt. In another bowl mix together the granulated sugar infused olive oil until the sugar is fully oiled. To that add the eggs, vanilla extract, lemon juice; stir until smooth, then fold in your dry ingredients until just incorporated.

Scoop a child's handful of dough and roll it into a ball. Then dab the top of the ball of dough into the bowl of lemon zest, dried basil and sugar until nicely crusted. Place the crusted cookie balls on the baking sheet. They will flatten on their own to about 2 inches in diameter. Bake for 11 minutes. Allow to cool briefly on the pan before sampling a warm cookie, then transfer to a wire rack to cool completely.

CHOCOLATE CHIP COOKIES

Whether you're winning the local bake sale or you want to try something different with the cookies for Santa, adding some Ginger Mint infused olive oil will add unique flavor to a classic chocolate chip cookie. The oil will concentrate its flavor more into the chocolate chips than the cookie bread.

- 2 cups of all purpose flour
- 1/2 teaspoon of baking soda
- 1 teaspoon of salt
- 3/4 cup of packed brown sugar
- 3/4 cup of granulated sugar
- 1-1/2 cup of unsweetened dark chocolate chips
- 1/2 cup of Ginger Mint infused olive oil
- 1 farm fresh egg
- 1 tablespoon of pure vanilla extract

Sift your dry ingredients together in a mixing bowl. Combine your wet ingredients in another bowl, then fold into the dry ingredients. Once incorporated, put the bowl in the freezer for about 20 minutes so the oil starts to gel. Preheat your oven to 350^0 F and line a baking sheet with parchment paper.

Use an ice cream scoop to gather something like a small ball of dough. The scoop works better than rolling with your hands because it doesn't warm up the oil as much. Place the dough ball on a seasoned cookie sheet, leaving about 2 inches between each cookie. You can press the ball down slightly with the bottom of a glass. Bake for 10 minutes, or until the tops are puffed and the edges are golden brown. Let them cool on the sheet for another 10 minutes before transferring to a wire rack.

SPICED ORANGE LOAF

A slice of this bread pairs very well with a hot coffee, favorite book, comfy chair and a rainy day.

- 1-1/2 cups of all purpose flour
- 1 tablespoon baking powder
- 1/2 teaspoon of salt
- 4 farm fresh eggs
- 3/4 cup of sugar
- 2/3 cup of Spiced Orange infused olive oil
- 1 orange, zested

Start by preheating your oven to 350⁰ F. Lightly oil and dust a loaf pan with flour. Beat the eggs in a bowl until the yolks and whites are fully integrated. Mix in the sugar, Spiced Orange infused olive oil, and the orange zest. In a separate bowl sift together the flour, baking powder, and. Combine everything gently; don't over mix or your bread will become more chewy. Pour your batter into the prepared loaf pan, dust the top with cinnamon sugar (optional) and bake for 45 minutes (or until a toothpick poked in the center comes out clean). Resist temptation and allow it to cool in the pan for 10 minutes, then remove it from the pan and cool fully on a wire rack.

APPLE CINNAMON POPOVERS

Popovers originally come from England, where they are called Yorkshire pudding, and typically served with roast beef and a savory gravy. In the USA we tend to make them more like a puff pastry, with fruit or sweet ingredients. If you don't have a popover pan, a regular muffin pan will also work.

- 1 cup of all purpose flour
- 1 teaspoon of salt
- 1 large apple
- 1 cup whole milk
- 2 tablespoons of dark honey
- 3 farm fresh eggs
- 3 tablespoons of Spiced Orange infused olive oil, divided
- 1 teaspoon of vanilla extract

Put your empty six muffin pan into your oven and preheat it to 450° F. Combine your flour and salt in a small bowl. In a large bowl whisk together the wet ingredients (except the olive oil) until well combined. Peel, core and dice a large apple and add it to your wet ingredients. Gently fold in your dry ingredients until smooth, being careful not to over stir.

Remove the hot muffin pan from the oven and quickly drop a half tablespoon of infused olive oil into each muffin cup, then fill it up halfway with the batter. Return to the oven and bake for 15 minutes, then reduce the temperature to 375° F and bake another 15 minutes. Don't open the door! The steam helps them puff. They should look golden brown through the window.

These are best served hot and fresh on a Saturday morning brunch, although you should probably wait 5 minutes after taking them out of the oven to avoid burning your mouth.

HOMEMADE ICE CREAM

While some people prefer to drizzle a fruited olive oils over their ice cream (and you totally can - just put it back in the freezer for 15 minutes to gel), this recipe is for making ice cream from scratch with olive oil in it.

- 3 cups of whole milk
- 1 teaspoon of salt
- 5 farm fresh egg yolks
- 1/2 cup of granulated sugar
- 1/3 cup of infused olive oil
- Add ins (fruit, chocolate, nuts, etc.)

Add the milk and salt to a pot and bring to a low simmer. While it is heating, in a mixing bowl vigorously whisk your egg yolks and sugar until the sugar is fully dissolved and it pours like a ribbon off your whisk. Once the milk is bubbling, slowly drizzle it into the mixing bowl so as to temper the eggs instead of scrambling them. Return the mixture to your pot on the stove, and stir until it has thickened enough to draw a line through it with your whisk.

Remove from the heat and add your favorite infused olive oil. Good flavors here are peppermint, star anise and cardamom, Spiced Orange, Ginger Mint, or vanilla bean. Whisk to incorporate, cover in an airtight container, and chill in the fridge for four hours. Put the mixer bowl you'll use later into the freezer too, so it's cold when you go to the next step.

Transfer the cooled mixture into a countertop stand mixer and use the paddle attachment to mix until thick. Add any solid ingredients you want at this point, such as berry compote, nuts, or chocolate nibs.

MOROCCAN SPICED ORANGES

This appetizer or dessert is common throughout the menus of Morocco. It is traditionally made with freshly toasted spices. We have adapted it to include the olive oil.

- 3 medium Navel oranges
- 3 tablespoons of raw honey
- 1/3 cup of Spiced Orange infused olive oil
- 1 tablespoon of white sesame seeds
- 1 tablespoon of black sesame seeds

Cut the peel and pith off the oranges, and slice them into 1/4 inch thick circles. Poke out any seeds. Warm the honey slightly in a microwave, and mix it with the olive oil in a bowl. Add the orange slices and toss to coat evenly. Allow to sit and marinate, at least 30 minutes up to overnight in the fridge. The oil might congeal slightly, but will melt at room temperature in a few minutes.

To serve, pour the liquid onto a platter, and arrange the slices on top. Lightly toast the sesame seeds on dry heat, mix, and sprinkle evenly.

Optional: try using blood oranges, or mandarins. The skin and pith on mandarins is thin enough that you don't have to peel them unless you want to.

ACKNOWLEDGEMENTS

IMAGE CREDITS AND DISCLAIMER

Most of the images in this book were generated using ChatGPT 4.0, an AI image creation tool provided by OpenAI. The authors own the rights to these images, subject to compliance with OpenAI's Content Policy and Terms of Service. Any resemblance to real persons, living or dead, or real places, events, or things is purely coincidental. All other images are attributed to or adapted from their source by the authors with reference.

THANK YOU

Thank you to all our customers and friends who have supported us along the way as we have made this little dream come true! There are a few specific people who we want to single out. If you happen to live in the Tri Cities area of Tennessee please give them your business. Thank you to Leah and Dan Bolton with Quantum Leap for being our very first customers. They have a great trampoline park and you should take your kids there. Thank you to our friends who tested our recipes and gave us feedback and suggestions: Matt Nordin (High Caliber Home Inspections), Choya Hardin (www.incredibletowns.com), and Stevianne Titus (steviannetitus.etsy.com). Thanks also to Tiffany with Stella Sourdough, Devin with Premier Appliance, Leslie with Faithful Fields Farms, Tammy Knapp with

Funny Farm, and Piere with Piere's Marketplace for getting us started in business to business sales. Thank you to our customers at the Kingsport and Bristol State Street farmers markets who got us started and proved to us that we have a marketable product. Thank you to Dan Toth at Mountain View Pure Water for your fellowship in Christ and introducing us to the world of reverse osmosis water.

ABOUT US

Ian was born and raised in Alaska, and Kesha was born and raised in Texas. We married in 2011, and live in the tri-cities area of eastern Tennessee.

Our dream was born during the summer of 2020, as we were walking our dog and chatting about the better world we would help create post-Covid. During those talks, we came up with the idea of a Bed and Breakfast Cafe that provided a venue where the five principles of an abundant life could flourish. We never expected that God would move us to eastern Tennessee just over two years later, and provide us the opportunity to start realizing that dream through the R&O Ranch, but here we are!

With your support, we look forward to continuing on this path, developing our talents to greater levels, and giving back to our community and nation. We appreciate you participating in this journey with us, and hope you benefit along the way.